little lawyers

A Kid's Guide to Becoming a Lawyer

sarah michaels

introduction

why become a lawyer?

Have you ever thought about standing up for justice, helping people in need, or solving tricky problems? If you answered "yes" to any of these questions, then becoming a lawyer might be the perfect career for you! In this section, we'll explore the many reasons why you might want to join the ranks of the world's greatest legal minds.

First of all, let's talk about the power of making a difference. Lawyers have a unique opportunity to help individuals, groups, and even entire communities. They can protect the rights of people who might not be able to defend themselves, and they can make sure that everyone is treated fairly under the law. Imagine using your skills and knowledge to change someone's life for the better, or even to shape the future of your country. As a lawyer, you can do just that!

Another great reason to become a lawyer is the chance to be a problem solver. Every day, lawyers tackle complex challenges and come up with creative solutions. They need to think critically, analyze situations from different perspectives, and find the best way to resolve disputes. If you love puzzles, riddles, or figuring out how things work, then you'll probably enjoy the intellectual challenges that come with being a lawyer.

Now, let's talk about the wide range of career options available to lawyers. Did you know that there are many different types of lawyers, each specializing in a specific area of law? Some lawyers work on criminal cases, defending people accused of crimes or prosecuting those who break the law. Others focus on civil law, helping people resolve disputes over contracts, property, or personal injury. There are also lawyers who work with businesses, governments, and non-profit organizations, advising them on legal matters and making sure they follow the rules. With so many options to choose from, you're sure to find a field of law that aligns with your passions and interests.

You might also be interested to know that a career in law can be financially rewarding. While it's true that many lawyers work long hours and face challenging situations, they are often well compensated for their hard work and dedication. As a lawyer, you can enjoy a comfortable lifestyle and provide for your family, all while doing something you love.

Of course, we can't forget about the amazing opportunities for personal growth and development that come with being a lawyer. In this profession, you'll never stop learning. The world of law is always changing, with new laws being passed and old ones being updated. To be successful, you'll need to stay informed about the latest developments and continue to hone your skills. This means that as a lawyer, you'll always be growing, adapting, and becoming the best version of yourself.

In addition to all of these benefits, being a lawyer can also be a lot of fun! You'll have the chance to meet interesting people, visit new places, and experience exciting situations that you might never have encountered otherwise. And with each new case, you'll have the opportunity to learn something new, whether it's about a different area of law, a unique aspect of human nature, or a fascinating piece of history.

Now that we've covered some of the reasons why you might want to become a lawyer, let's take a moment to think about what it really means to be one. A lawyer is someone who has a deep understanding of the law and uses that knowledge to help others. They are skilled communicators, able to listen carefully and express their ideas clearly. They are also passionate about justice and committed to making the world a better place.

If you think you have what it takes to be a lawyer, then you're in for an exciting and rewarding journey. Throughout this book, we'll help you explore the many aspects of the legal profession, from the skills you'll need to develop, to the different types of law you can specialize in. We'll also take a look at the steps you'll need to follow to become a lawyer, from high school all the way to law school and beyond. And finally, we'll share some tips and advice on how to succeed in your legal career and make the most of your unique talents.

But remember, becoming a lawyer isn't just about the prestige, the money, or even the thrill of solving complex problems. It's about using your skills and knowledge to make a positive impact on the lives of others. As you read through this book and learn more about the world of law, keep in mind the many ways in which you can use your future legal expertise to help people, fight for justice, and create a better world.

So, are you ready to embark on this incredible adventure? Are you excited to explore the fascinating world of law and discover the many ways you can make a difference? If the answer is "yes," then you're in the right place! Together, we'll journey through the ins and outs of becoming a lawyer, and by the time you finish this book, you'll have a clear understanding of what it takes to join the ranks of history's greatest legal minds.

As we move forward, remember that you're never too young to start dreaming big and setting goals for your future. And who knows? One day, you might be the one standing in a courtroom, fighting for justice, and making a lasting impact on the world. With determination, hard work, and a passion for helping others, you can achieve your dreams and become an amazing lawyer.

Now, let's dive into the exciting world of law and start this journey together. We'll begin by exploring the essential skills that every aspiring lawyer needs to develop. From reading and writing to public speaking and critical thinking, we'll help you build a strong foundation that will prepare you for success in your future legal career. So, grab your detective hat and your magnifying glass, and let's start investigating the amazing world of law!

different types of lawyers

Now that you're excited about the world of law, let's take a closer look at the different types of lawyers out there. After all, not all lawyers do the same thing, and it's important to find the area of law that interests you the most. Are you ready to explore the many fascinating specialties in the legal profession? Let's dive in!

1. Criminal Lawyers

Do you enjoy watching crime shows or reading mystery novels? If so, you might be interested in becoming a criminal lawyer. These lawyers work on cases involving crimes, like theft, assault, or even murder. Criminal lawyers can be divided into two categories: defense attorneys and prosecutors.

Defense attorneys represent people who have been accused of committing a crime. Their job is to ensure that their clients receive a fair trial and that their rights are protected. They work hard to build a strong defense for their clients and to argue their case in court.

On the other hand, prosecutors represent the government in criminal cases. They work to prove that the person accused of a crime is guilty, and they seek to ensure that justice is served. Prosecutors can work at the local, state, or federal level, depending on the type of crime involved.

2. Civil Lawyers

If you're more interested in helping people resolve disputes and disagreements, you might want to consider becoming a civil lawyer. Civil law covers a wide range of issues, such as contracts, property, and personal injury. Civil lawyers help their clients navigate the legal system and seek solutions to their problems, which can involve going to court or negotiating settlements.

Some civil lawyers specialize in specific areas, such as family law, which deals with issues like divorce, child custody, and adoption. Others might focus on employment law, helping workers and employers resolve disputes over workplace rights and responsibilities.

3. Corporate Lawyers

Are you intrigued by the world of business and finance? If so, a career as a corporate lawyer might be right up your alley. Corporate lawyers work with companies, advising them on legal matters related to their operations. This can include drafting contracts, ensuring compliance with regulations, and protecting intellectual property rights.

Corporate lawyers can work in-house, meaning they are employed directly by the company they represent, or they can work for a law firm that provides legal services to multiple clients. Some corporate lawyers even specialize in specific industries, such as technology, healthcare, or entertainment.

4. Intellectual Property Lawyers

Do you have a creative side and a passion for innovation? Intellectual property lawyers work with clients to protect their inventions, artistic works, and brand identities. They help clients secure patents for new inventions, register trademarks for brand names and logos, and protect copyrights for books, movies, and music.

Intellectual property lawyers also help clients enforce their rights, which can involve taking legal action against those who steal or copy their work. If you love the idea of helping creators and inventors protect their valuable creations, this could be the perfect legal specialty for you.

5. Environmental Lawyers

If you're passionate about protecting the planet and preserving natural resources, you might want to consider a career as an environmental lawyer. These lawyers work with clients and government agencies to ensure compliance with environmental laws and regulations. They might help clients obtain permits for new projects, defend against allegations of environmental harm, or advocate for stronger environmental protections.

Environmental lawyers can work for government agencies, non-profit organizations, or private law firms, and they often collaborate with scientists, engineers, and other experts to address complex environmental issues.

6. Immigration Lawyers

Do you have a heart for helping people from

different cultures and backgrounds? Immigration lawyers assist clients with matters related to immigration, citizenship, and visas. They help individuals and families navigate the complex immigration system and work to ensure that their clients can legally live, work, or study in a new country. Immigration lawyers might help clients apply for visas, represent them in deportation proceedings, or assist employers in hiring foreign workers.

Immigration lawyers often have a deep understanding of international law and the unique challenges faced by immigrants. They can work for law firms, non-profit organizations, or even government agencies that deal with immigration matters.

7. Personal Injury Lawyers

If you're interested in helping people who have been injured or harmed, you might want to explore a career as a personal injury lawyer. These lawyers represent clients who have been hurt in accidents, such as car crashes, workplace incidents, or medical malpractice cases. They work to help their clients receive compensation for their injuries and losses, which can include medical expenses, lost wages, and pain and suffering.

Personal injury lawyers often work on a contingency fee basis, which means they only get paid if their client receives a settlement or a favorable verdict in court. This can make their work especially rewarding, as they are directly helping people in need.

8. Human Rights Lawyers

Are you passionate about social justice and fighting for the rights of the vulnerable? Human rights lawyers work to protect the rights and freedoms of individuals and groups who are facing discrimination, oppression, or violence. They might represent clients in court, advocate for new laws and policies, or work with international organizations to promote human rights around the world.

Human rights lawyers can work for non-profit organizations, government agencies, or private law firms, and they often collaborate with activists, community leaders, and other professionals to bring about positive change.

As you can see, there are many different types of lawyers, each with their unique focus and areas of expertise. It's important to find the area of law that interests you the most and aligns with your passions and values. Remember, as a lawyer, you have the opportunity to make a significant impact on the lives of others and on society as a whole.

the role of lawyers in society

Let's take a closer look at the essential role that lawyers play in our society. From protecting individual rights to shaping public policy, lawyers have a significant impact on the world around us. Are you ready to discover how lawyers help make our world a better, fairer place? Let's get started!

1. Upholding the Rule of Law

One of the most important roles that lawyers play in society is upholding the rule of law. The rule of law is the idea that everyone, no matter who they are, should be treated fairly and equally under the law. Lawyers help ensure that our legal system remains fair and just by representing clients, advocating for their rights, and working to improve the law itself.

By upholding the rule of law, lawyers help create a society where people can trust that their rights will be protected, and where everyone has an opportunity to succeed. This makes the work of lawyers essential to maintaining a safe, stable, and prosperous society.

2. Defending Individual Rights

Another crucial role that lawyers play in society is defending individual rights. Every person has certain rights, such as the right to free speech, the right to privacy, and the right to a fair trial. Lawyers work tirelessly to protect these rights and to ensure that everyone is treated fairly under the law.

For example, a criminal defense attorney might represent someone who has been accused of a crime, ensuring that their client receives a fair trial and that their rights are protected throughout the legal process. Likewise, a human rights lawyer might work to defend the rights of a vulnerable group, such as refugees or victims of discrimination.

3. Resolving Disputes

Lawyers also play an essential role in resolving disputes, both between individuals and between organizations. Disputes can arise over a wide range of issues, such as contracts, property, or personal injury. When these disputes arise, lawyers help their clients navigate the legal system, negotiate settlements, or represent them in court.

By resolving disputes, lawyers help maintain peace and stability in our society. They ensure that conflicts are resolved fairly and peacefully, rather than through violence or other harmful means.

4. Shaping Public Policy

Did you know that lawyers also play a significant role in shaping public policy? Many lawyers work with government agencies, non-profit organizations, or other groups to advocate for new laws and policies that will improve our society. They might draft legislation, testify before government committees, or work behind the scenes to influence policymakers.

Some lawyers even run for public office or serve as judges, using their legal expertise to make important decisions that affect our lives. By shaping public policy, lawyers have the opportunity to create lasting, positive change in our society.

5. Educating the Public

Lawyers also play a crucial role in educating the public about the law and their rights. They might speak at schools, write articles, or give presentations to help people better understand the legal system and their rights within it.

By educating the public, lawyers empower individuals to stand up for their rights and to make informed decisions about their lives. This knowledge helps create a society where people can confidently navigate the legal system and participate in the democratic process.

As we can see, the role of lawyers in society is both vast and essential. They work tirelessly to uphold the rule of law, defend individual rights, resolve disputes, shape public policy, and educate the public. In doing so, lawyers help create a fair, just, and prosperous society for all of us.

Now that you have a better understanding of the important role lawyers play in our society, you might be even more excited about the idea of joining their ranks. In the upcoming sections, we'll explore the legal system in more detail, as well as learn about important legal concepts and the many steps you'll need to take to become a lawyer. With each new discovery, you'll be one step closer to finding your perfect legal career path and making a difference in the world.

As you continue your journey through this book, remember that, as a lawyer, you have the power to shape the world around you and improve the lives of countless people. Whether you choose to work in criminal law, civil law, or any of the other fascinating legal specialties we've discussed, you'll be making a lasting, positive impact on our society.

Keep this in mind as you explore the world of law and envision the type of lawyer you want to become. With passion, hard work, and dedication, you can achieve your dreams and become an amazing lawyer who makes a real difference in the world.

fun facts about famous lawyers in history

By now, you're probably eager to learn even more about the world of law and the people who have shaped it. In this section, we'll take a journey back in time to discover some fun facts about famous lawyers in history. These trailblazers have made significant contributions to the legal profession, and their stories might just inspire you as you pursue your own legal dreams. Ready to embark on this exciting historical adventure? Let's go!

1. Abraham Lincoln: Honest Abe, the Lawyer

Before becoming the 16th President of the United States and one of the most admired leaders in American history, Abraham Lincoln was a lawyer. He practiced law for nearly 25 years in Illinois and earned a reputation for his honesty and integrity, which earned him the nickname "Honest Abe." Fun fact: Lincoln didn't attend law school but instead taught himself by reading law books borrowed from a fellow lawyer!

2. Thurgood Marshall: A Civil Rights Trailblazer

Thurgood Marshall was the first African-American Supreme Court Justice, serving from 1967 to 1991. Before his appointment to the Supreme Court, Marshall was a prominent civil rights lawyer. He famously argued the landmark case Brown v. Board of Education before the Supreme Court, which led to the desegregation of public schools in the United States. Fun fact: Marshall was known for his sense of humor, and he loved to tell stories and jokes to his colleagues on the Supreme Court!

3. Ruth Bader Ginsburg: The Notorious RBG

Ruth Bader Ginsburg, affectionately known as the

"Notorious RBG," was the second female Supreme Court Justice, serving from 1993 until her passing in 2020. Before joining the Supreme Court, Ginsburg was a pioneering lawyer in the fight for gender equality. She co-founded the Women's Rights Project at the American Civil Liberties Union (ACLU) and argued several groundbreaking cases before the Supreme Court. Fun fact: Ginsburg was known for her love of opera, and she even appeared as an extra in a few opera productions!

4. Mahatma Gandhi: A Lawyer Turned Freedom Fighter

Before becoming the leader of the Indian independence movement and an icon of nonviolent resistance, Mahatma Gandhi was a lawyer. He studied law in England and began his legal career in South Africa, where he first became involved in the fight for civil rights. Gandhi's legal background played a significant role in shaping his philosophy of nonviolent protest and his approach to achieving social change. Fun fact: Gandhi was known for his simple lifestyle, which included wearing homespun clothing and practicing vegetarianism.

5. John Adams: A Founding Father and Lawyer

John Adams, the second President of the United States, was also a lawyer by profession. Before his political career, Adams practiced law in Massachusetts and was known for his passionate defense of individual rights. He famously defended the British soldiers accused of murder in the Boston Massacre, believing that they deserved a fair trial, even though it was an unpopular position to take. Fun fact: Adams was a prolific writer, and many of his letters and writings have been preserved, providing valuable insights into the founding of the United States.

6. Nelson Mandela: From Lawyer to President

Nelson Mandela, the first black president of South Africa and a global symbol of the fight against apartheid, began his career as a lawyer. Mandela opened the first black law firm in South Africa with his friend and fellow lawyer, Oliver Tambo. Their firm provided affordable legal services to black South Africans who faced discrimination under apartheid laws. Fun fact: Mandela loved boxing, and he often used it as a way to stay physically and mentally fit during his long years of imprisonment on Robben Island.

7. Clara Shortridge Foltz: A Trailblazer for Women in Law

Clara Shortridge Foltz was the first female lawyer on the West Coast of the United States and a trailblazer for women in the legal profession. After her husband abandoned her and their five children, Foltz decided to study law and become an attorney to support her family. She faced many challenges along the way, including having to change California law to allow women to practice law! Fun fact: Foltz was also a suffragist and a journalist, and she even ran for governor of California in 1930!

8. Sir William Blackstone: The Author of the Famous Commentaries

Sir William Blackstone was an influential English jurist and legal scholar whose work has had a significant impact on the development of law, particularly in the United States. His most famous work, "Commentaries on the Laws of England," was a comprehensive and accessible guide to English law, and it became a primary legal reference for American lawyers and judges in the late 18th and early 19th centuries. Fun fact: Blackstone was also a talented musician and composer, and he wrote several operas!

As we've seen, lawyers have played important roles throughout history, shaping societies and fighting for justice in various ways. These famous lawyers have left lasting legacies that continue to inspire and guide the legal profession today. As you pursue your dreams of becoming a lawyer, remember that you, too, have the potential to make a significant impact on the world and the lives of others.

1 /
building a strong foundation

skills needed to become a successful lawyer

BY NOW, you might be feeling inspired by the famous lawyers we've learned about and eager to pursue your own path in the legal profession. But what skills do you need to become a successful lawyer? In this section, we'll explore the key skills and qualities that can help you excel in the world of law. Ready to discover what it takes to be a great lawyer? Let's dive in!

1. Strong Communication Skills

One of the most important skills for a lawyer is the ability to communicate effectively, both in writing and verbally. Lawyers need to be able to clearly explain complex legal concepts to their clients, persuade judges and juries, and create compelling written documents, such as contracts or briefs. To develop strong communication skills, practice speaking in front of others, join a debate team, or take writing classes.

2. Analytical and Critical Thinking Skills

Lawyers often need to analyze large amounts of information, identify important details, and draw logical conclusions. Developing strong analytical and critical thinking skills can help you excel in the legal profession. You can hone these skills by engaging in activities like solving puzzles, playing strategy games, and participating in discussions or debates that challenge your thinking.

3. Research Skills

Being a lawyer often requires extensive research to gather facts, find relevant laws, and analyze past cases. Strong research skills are essential for a successful legal career. To build your research skills, try joining a school research project, volunteering at a library, or participating in a mock trial competition.

4. Attention to Detail

Attention to detail is a crucial skill for lawyers, as even small mistakes can have significant consequences in legal matters. Whether you're reviewing a contract or preparing a court document, it's important to be thorough and meticulous. To improve your attention to detail, practice proofreading your own work or try activities that require precision, like painting or model building.

5. Time Management and Organization

Lawyers often juggle multiple cases and deadlines, making time management and organization essential skills. Learning to prioritize tasks, create schedules, and manage your time effectively can help you succeed in the fast-paced world of law. To develop these skills, try using a planner, setting personal deadlines for projects, or participating in extracurricular activities that require time management.

6. Empathy and Compassion

While not always thought of as a traditional "skill," empathy and compassion are important qualities for lawyers. Understanding and empathizing with your clients' situations can help you better advocate for their needs and build strong relationships. To cultivate empathy and compassion, practice active listening, volunteer in your community, or engage in activities that expose you to diverse perspectives.

7. Negotiation Skills

Whether you're settling a dispute, advocating for a client's interests, or resolving a legal issue, negotiation skills are essential for many lawyers. Being able to find common ground, compromise, and persuade others can help you achieve successful outcomes for your clients. To develop your negotiation skills, try participating in mock negotiations, joining a debate team, or practicing negotiation techniques with friends or family members.

8. Adaptability and Flexibility

The world of law is constantly changing, and lawyers need to be adaptable and flexible to stay ahead. Being open to new ideas, embracing change, and quickly adjusting to new situations can help you excel in your legal career. To build your adaptability and flexibility, seek out new experiences, challenge yourself to learn new skills, and practice problem-solving in unfamiliar situations.

9. Perseverance and Resilience

Becoming a successful lawyer often requires perseverance and resilience in the face of challenges, setbacks, or even failures. Learning to bounce back from difficult situations and stay focused on your goals is an important quality for a lawyer. To develop perseverance and resilience, set challenging goals for yourself, practice self-reflection, and seek out support from friends, family, or mentors when faced with obstacles.

10. Teamwork and Collaboration

While lawyers sometimes work independently, they also frequently collaborate with colleagues, clients, and other professionals. Being able to work effectively in a team, share ideas, and communicate clearly with others is an important skill for a successful legal career. To enhance your teamwork and collaboration abilities, participate in group projects, join clubs or sports teams, or engage in other activities that require working with others.

11. Ethical Decision-Making

Lawyers are often faced with complex ethical dilemmas and must make decisions that uphold the principles of justice and fairness. Developing strong ethical decision-making skills can help you navigate these challenges and maintain your integrity as a lawyer. To strengthen your ethical decision-making abilities, study professional ethics, engage in discussions about moral dilemmas, or seek out mentors who can offer guidance and advice.

As you can see, becoming a successful lawyer requires a diverse set of skills and qualities. By working to develop these skills now, you'll be better prepared for the challenges and opportunities that await you in the legal profession. Remember, practice makes perfect, and even the most accomplished lawyers had to start somewhere!

extracurricular activities and clubs to join

You're probably excited to start developing the skills and qualities needed for a successful legal career. But where can you find opportunities to practice and refine these skills outside of the classroom? In this section, we'll explore a variety of extracurricular activities and clubs that can help you become a well-rounded, confident, and skilled future lawyer. Are you ready to dive into the world of fun and enriching activities? Let's get started!

1. Debate Team or Club

Joining a debate team or club is an excellent way to develop your communication, critical thinking, and persuasion skills. Debating requires you to research and understand various topics, form logical arguments, and present your ideas confidently and convincingly. Plus, it's a great way to meet new friends who share your passion for lively discussions and intellectual challenges!

2. Mock Trial

Mock trial competitions give you the chance to step into the shoes of a lawyer and experience the excitement of a real courtroom. You'll learn about courtroom procedures, legal terminology, and the art of crafting compelling arguments. Participating in mock trial will help you develop your public speaking, critical thinking, and teamwork skills, all while having a blast!

3. Model United Nations (MUN)

Model United Nations (MUN) is an educational simulation where students role-play as delegates to the United Nations and participate in debates, negotiations, and the drafting of resolutions. MUN is an excellent way to improve your research, public speaking, negotiation, and diplomacy skills. Plus, you'll learn about global issues and the inner workings of international organizations.

4. Student Government

Getting involved in student government is a fantastic opportunity to develop your leadership, teamwork, and communication skills. As a student government representative, you'll help make decisions that affect your school community, plan events, and work closely with your peers and school administrators. This experience can be valuable preparation for a future career in law, as lawyers often take on leadership roles and work with diverse groups of people.

5. Volunteering and Community Service

Volunteering in your community can help you develop empathy, compassion, and a strong sense of civic responsibility – all important qualities for a lawyer. Plus, volunteering allows you to explore different fields and causes, which may help you discover the areas of law that interest you most. Some great places to volunteer include local nonprofits, schools, animal shelters, or community centers.

6. Writing or Journalism Clubs

Strong writing skills are essential for a successful legal career, and joining a writing or journalism club is a great way to practice and improve your writing. You might contribute to your school newspaper, write short stories or essays, or even participate in writing competitions. Writing clubs can also help you develop your creativity, critical thinking, and attention to detail.

7. Drama or Theater Clubs

Participating in drama or theater clubs can help you develop your public speaking and presentation skills, as well as build your confidence in front of an audience. Plus, acting can be a fun way to explore different perspectives and learn about empathy – an important quality for a lawyer.

8. Language Clubs

Learning a second (or third!) language can be a valuable asset for a lawyer, especially if you're interested in international law or working with diverse communities. Joining a language club can help you practice your language skills, learn about different cultures, and make new friends from around the world.

9. Chess Club

Chess is a strategic game that requires critical thinking, problem-solving, and the ability to anticipate your opponent's moves – all skills that can be helpful for a lawyer. Joining a chess club can be a fun way to challenge your brain, meet new friends, and improve your analytical abilities.

10. Environmental or Social Justice Clubs

If you're passionate about making a difference and standing up for important causes, consider joining an environmental or social justice club. These clubs focus on raising awareness, advocating for change, and taking action to address various issues, such as climate change, human rights, or equality. Participating in these clubs can help you develop your advocacy skills, learn about different areas of law, and make a positive impact on your community.

11. Entrepreneurship or Business Clubs

Many lawyers work with businesses or even start their own law firms. Joining an entrepreneurship or business club can help you learn about business principles, develop your leadership skills, and gain experience working on projects with a team. Plus, it's an excellent opportunity to explore different areas of law, such as corporate or intellectual property law.

12. Art or Music Clubs

While art or music clubs might not seem directly related to a legal career, participating in these activities can help you develop important skills like attention to detail, creativity, and patience. Plus, engaging in creative pursuits can provide a valuable outlet for stress and a way to maintain a healthy work-life balance – something that's important for lawyers and aspiring lawyers alike!

As you can see, there are plenty of extracurricular activities and clubs that can help you develop the skills and qualities needed for a successful legal career. Don't be afraid to try new things and step out of your comfort zone. The more experiences you have, the more well-rounded and prepared you'll be for the exciting world of law.

exploring law-related books, movies, and tv shows

You're well on your way to becoming a fantastic lawyer, but sometimes, it's nice to take a break from studying and extracurricular activities to relax and enjoy some entertainment. The good news is that you can still learn about the world of law and feed your passion for justice by exploring law-related books, movies, and TV shows. In this section, we'll share some fantastic recommendations that are not only enter- taining but also informative and inspiring. Ready to discover some exciting legal adventures? Let's dive in!

Books

1. "Theodore Boone: Kid Lawyer" by John Grisham

John Grisham is famous for his legal thrillers, and this book is perfect for young readers who want to explore the world of law. Follow the adventures of Theodore Boone, a 13-year-old who dreams of becoming a lawyer, as he gets caught up in a high-stakes murder trial that will test his courage and determination.

2. "The Wright 3" by Blue Balliett

This engaging mystery novel follows three friends who must use their problem-solving skills to solve an art-related mystery and save a historic building from demolition. Along the way, they learn about the legal system and the importance of preservation and community activism.

3. "The Lemonade Crime" by Jacqueline Davies

In this sequel to "The Lemonade War," siblings Evan and Jessie must use their knowledge of the legal system to prove that a classmate stole their hard-earned lemonade stand money. This fun and educational book introduces young readers to the concepts of fairness, justice, and the judicial process.

Movies

1. Legally Blonde (2001)

This entertaining and empowering movie follows Elle Woods, a fashion-conscious sorority girl who enrolls at Harvard Law School to win back her ex-boyfriend. Along the way, Elle discovers her true passion for law and becomes a successful and respected lawyer. While the movie is lighthearted and fun, it also teaches important lessons about self-confidence, perseverance, and the power of knowledge.

2. To Kill a Mockingbird (1962)

Based on the classic novel by Harper Lee, this film tells the story of a small-town lawyer, Atticus Finch, who defends a Black man accused of a crime he didn't commit in the racially charged South during the 1930s. The movie explores themes of justice, morality, and standing up for what's right, making it a powerful and thought-provoking watch.

3. The Mighty Ducks (1992)

In this heartwarming and funny movie, a successful lawyer named Gordon Bombay is sentenced to community service after a DUI and ends up coaching a ragtag youth hockey team. While not a traditional law-related movie, "The Mighty Ducks" teaches valuable lessons about teamwork, leadership, and the importance of giving back to the community.

TV Shows

1. Matilda and the Ramsay Bunch (2016-2018)

This British children's television series follows the life of Matilda Ramsay, the daughter of celebrity chef Gordon Ramsay, and her family. In one episode,

Matilda explores a career in law and learns about the legal system from a real-life lawyer. The show is a fun and educational way for young viewers to learn about different careers, including law.

2. The Fresh Prince of Bel-Air (1990-1996)

This popular sitcom follows the life of Will Smith, a teenager from a low-income neighborhood in Philadelphia who moves in with his wealthy aunt and uncle in the posh neighborhood of Bel-Air. Throughout the series, Will's cousin Hilary Banks pursues a career in law and attends law school, providing a glimpse into the challenges and rewards of a legal education. The show is both entertaining and educational, teaching valuable life lessons while exploring various aspects of law.

3. Just Add Magic (2015-2019)

This magical family-friendly show follows three friends who discover an enchanted cookbook that reveals mysterious recipes with magical effects. In one episode, the girls use a recipe to get a glimpse into their future careers, and one of them sees herself as a successful lawyer. The show encourages young viewers to dream big and pursue their passions, including the possibility of a career in law.

Podcasts

1. The Radio Adventures of Dr. Floyd

This fun and educational podcast series follows the

time-traveling adventures of Dr. Floyd and his companions as they visit important historical events and meet famous figures from the past. Several episodes touch on legal themes, such as the trials of famous outlaws, landmark Supreme Court decisions, and the drafting of the Constitution. The podcast is a great way for young listeners to learn about history and the legal system in an engaging and entertaining format.

2. Brains On!

"Brains On!" is a science podcast for kids that covers a wide range of fascinating topics. Some episodes touch on legal themes, such as intellectual property, animal rights, and the science of forensic investigations. By exploring the intersection of law and science, young listeners can gain a deeper understanding of the role of law in society and the importance of evidence-based decision-making.

As you can see, there are plenty of law-related books, movies, TV shows, and podcasts to keep you entertained and informed as you continue your journey to becoming a lawyer. By exploring these different forms of media, you can gain a broader understanding of the legal world, learn about important legal concepts, and discover inspiring stories of people who have made a difference in the pursuit of justice.

So, grab some popcorn, find a cozy spot, and enjoy these fantastic law-related adventures. Who knows? You might just find the inspiration you need to achieve your dreams and make a lasting impact on the world as a future lawyer!

2 /
understanding
the law

introduction to the legal system

HEY THERE, future lawyers! By now, you've learned about different types of lawyers, the skills needed to become successful in the field, and even some fun and interesting law-related entertainment. Now it's time to delve deeper into the fascinating world of law and explore the legal system itself. In this section, we'll give you a beginner's guide to the legal system, helping you understand its key components and how they work together to ensure fairness, justice, and order in our society. Are you ready to take your first steps into the world of law? Let's get started!

1. The Legal System: An Overview

The legal system is a complex network of laws, regulations, and institutions that help to maintain order, protect the rights of individuals, and ensure that justice is served. At its core, the legal system is based on the principle of the rule of law, which means that everyone, regardless of their background or social status, is subject to the same laws and entitled to the same legal protections. This principle is essential for ensuring fairness, accountability, and equality in our society.

2. Sources of Law

In order to understand the legal system, it's important to know where laws come from. Laws can be divided into two main categories: statutory law and common law.

Statutory law refers to laws that are created by legislatures, such as the United States Congress or state legislatures. These laws are also known as acts, statutes, or codes, and they can cover a wide range of topics, from criminal offenses to environmental regulations.

Common law, on the other hand, is based on the decisions made by judges in court cases. When a judge makes a decision in a case, that decision becomes a legal precedent, which can then be used as a guide for future cases involving similar issues. Over time, these precedents build up to form a body of law known as common law.

3. The Three Branches of Government

In the United States, the legal system is closely connected to the structure of the government, which is divided into three separate branches: the legislative, the executive, and the judicial.

The legislative branch is responsible for making laws. In the United States, this branch includes the United States Congress, which is made up of the House of Representatives and the Senate. At the state level, the legislative branch includes state legislatures.

The executive branch is responsible for enforcing laws. This branch includes the President of the United States, who is the head of the executive branch at the federal level, and the governors, who serve as the heads of the executive branch at the state level. The executive branch also includes various agencies and departments that help to carry out the enforcement of laws, such as the Department of Justice and the Environmental Protection Agency.

The judicial branch is responsible for interpreting laws and ensuring that they are applied fairly and consistently. This branch includes the court system, which is made up of various levels of courts, from the local and state courts all the way up to the United States Supreme Court.

4. The Court System

The court system plays a crucial role in the legal system, as it is responsible for resolving disputes, interpreting laws, and ensuring that justice is served. In the United States, there are two main types of courts: federal courts and state courts.

Federal courts hear cases that involve federal laws, disputes between states, and cases involving the United States Constitution. The federal court system is divided into three levels: district courts, appellate courts, and the United States Supreme Court.

State courts, on the other hand, hear cases that involve state laws and disputes between individuals within a state. The state court system is also divided into various levels, including trial courts, intermediate appellate courts, and state supreme courts.

5. The Legal Process

The legal process is the series of steps that are followed to resolve disputes, enforce laws, and ensure justice is served. While the specific details of the legal process can vary depending on the type of case and the jurisdiction, the general stages of the process include:

- Filing a complaint or lawsuit: When a person or organization believes that their rights have been violated or that they have been harmed by the actions of another party, they can file a complaint or lawsuit in court, seeking justice or compensation for their losses.

- Pretrial proceedings: Before a case goes to trial, there are various pretrial proceedings that take place. These can include the exchange of evidence and information between the parties (known as discovery), negotiations to settle the case out of court, and pretrial motions to resolve legal issues and disputes.

- Trial: If a case is not settled during the pretrial stage, it will proceed to trial. During the trial, both sides present evidence and arguments to a judge or jury, who will then make a decision based on the facts and the law.

- Appeal: After the trial, either party can appeal the decision to a higher court if they believe that there were errors made during the trial or that the law was not applied correctly. The appellate court will review the case and may uphold the original decision, reverse it, or order a new trial.

- Enforcement: Once a final decision has been made, the appropriate actions must be taken to enforce the judgment, such as the payment of damages or the enforcement of a court order.

The legal system is designed to provide a fair and orderly process for resolving disputes and enforcing laws. As a future lawyer, you'll play an essential role in this system, helping to protect the rights of individuals and ensure that justice is served.

important legal concepts

As you continue your journey into the fascinating world of law, it's essential to familiarize yourself with some key legal concepts that you'll encounter throughout your legal education and career. In this section, we'll introduce you to some of these important legal ideas, providing you with a strong foundation to build upon as you delve deeper into the world of law. Let's get started!

1. Presumption of Innocence

The presumption of innocence is a fundamental principle in the criminal justice system. It means that everyone accused of a crime is considered innocent until proven guilty. This principle helps ensure that defendants receive a fair trial, and it places the burden of proof on the prosecution. The prosecution must present enough evidence to prove the defendant's guilt beyond a reasonable doubt. If they cannot do this, the defendant is found not guilty.

2. Separation of Powers

As you learned in the previous section, the United States government is divided into three branches: the legislative, executive, and judicial branches. The separation of powers is a crucial concept that helps maintain a balance of power among these branches. Each branch has specific responsibilities and powers, and they also have the ability to check and balance the powers of the other branches. This system prevents any single branch from becoming too powerful and helps to protect the rights and liberties of the citizens.

3. Due Process

Due process is a legal principle that guarantees every person the right to fair and equal treatment under the law. It applies to both criminal and civil cases and ensures that individuals have the opportunity to be heard, the right to notice of legal proceedings against them, and the right to a fair and impartial trial. Due process helps protect the rights of individuals and promotes fairness and justice within the legal system.

4. Habeas Corpus

Habeas corpus is a legal principle that protects individuals from being unlawfully detained or imprisoned. The term "habeas corpus" is Latin for "you shall have the body," and it refers to a court order that requires a person being held in custody to be brought before a judge. The judge will then determine if the detention is lawful. If the detention is found to be unlawful, the individual must be released. This important legal concept helps protect individual liberties and prevent the government from detaining people without just cause.

5. Double Jeopardy

Double jeopardy is a legal principle that prohibits a

person from being tried twice for the same crime. This protection is provided by the Fifth Amendment to the United States Constitution, and it prevents the government from subjecting a person to multiple trials and punishments for the same offense. If a defendant is found not guilty in a criminal trial, they cannot be retried for the same crime, even if new evidence emerges.

6. Miranda Rights

You may have heard the phrase "You have the right to remain silent" on TV shows or movies. These words are part of the Miranda Rights, which are a set of legal rights that must be explained to a person who is being arrested and questioned by the police. The Miranda Rights come from a 1966 Supreme Court case, Miranda v. Arizona, and they help protect individuals' rights during interactions with law enforcement. These rights include the right to remain silent, the right to an attorney, and the right to have an attorney appointed if the individual cannot afford one.

7. Judicial Review

Judicial review is the power of the courts to review laws and government actions to determine whether they are constitutional. This important legal concept was established in the 1803 Supreme Court case Marbury v. Madison and helps maintain the balance of power among the branches of government. If a court finds that a law or government action is unconstitutional, it can declare that law or action invalid.

Now that you have a basic understanding of these important legal concepts, you're well on your way to becoming an informed and well-prepared future lawyer. Remember, these concepts are the building blocks of the legal system, and they play a crucial role in ensuring fairness, justice, and the protection of individual rights.

As you continue to explore the world of law, you'll encounter these concepts in various contexts, from court cases and legislation to legal debates and discussions. By understanding these principles, you'll be better equipped to analyze complex legal issues and apply your knowledge to real-world situations.

So, future legal eagles, keep these legal concepts in mind as you continue your journey into the captivating world of law. Use your newfound knowledge to spark discussions with your friends, family, and teachers, and don't hesitate to ask questions and seek further information on topics that interest you. Your curiosity and passion for learning will be your greatest assets as you forge your path to becoming a successful lawyer.

Always remember that the legal system is built upon these fundamental principles, and as a future lawyer, you'll play a vital role in upholding and promoting these values. Your dedication to justice, fairness, and the protection of individual rights will not only benefit your future clients but also contribute to the betterment of society as a whole.

the constitution and bill of rights

One of the most important documents you'll encounter on your journey is the United States Constitution, along with its first ten amendments, known as the Bill of Rights. In this section, we'll dive into the Constitution and Bill of Rights, exploring their significance and the role they play in shaping our legal system. Are you ready? Let's go!

The United States Constitution

The Constitution is the supreme law of the land and serves as the foundation for the entire American legal system. It was written in 1787 and ratified by the states in 1788. The Constitution established the structure of the federal government, defined the powers of the three branches of government (executive, legislative, and judicial), and outlined the basic rights and liberties of the American people.

The Constitution is divided into three main parts: the Preamble, the Articles, and the Amendments. The Preamble is the introduction and sets forth the purpose of the document. The Articles describe the structure and powers of the federal government, and the Amendments include changes and additions to the Constitution. There are currently 27 amendments to the Constitution, with the first ten being known as the Bill of Rights.

The Bill of Rights

The Bill of Rights is a collection of the first ten amendments to the United States Constitution. These amendments were added to the Constitution in 1791, just a few years after it was ratified. The purpose of the Bill of Rights was to protect the individual liberties of American citizens and limit the power of the federal government. Let's take a closer look at each of the ten amendments that make up the Bill of Rights.

1. First Amendment: The First Amendment protects the freedom of speech, religion, press, assembly, and petition. This amendment guarantees that the government cannot interfere with these essential rights, allowing individuals to express their opinions, practice their religion, and gather peacefully without fear of government retaliation.

2. Second Amendment: The Second Amendment protects the right to keep and bear arms. This amendment was included to ensure that individuals have the ability to defend themselves and their property.

3. Third Amendment: The Third Amendment prevents the government from forcing citizens to house

soldiers in their homes during times of peace without their consent.

4. Fourth Amendment: The Fourth Amendment protects individuals from unreasonable searches and seizures. This means that the government cannot search a person's property or take their belongings without a warrant, which is a legal document issued by a judge.

5. Fifth Amendment: The Fifth Amendment provides several protections for individuals accused of crimes, including the right to remain silent, protection from double jeopardy, and the guarantee of due process.

6. Sixth Amendment: The Sixth Amendment ensures the right to a fair and speedy trial in criminal cases. This includes the right to an impartial jury, the right to be informed of the charges against you, and the right to confront witnesses and have legal repre-sentation.

7. Seventh Amendment: The Seventh Amendment guarantees the right to a jury trial in civil cases, which are disputes between individuals or organizations, rather than criminal cases.

8. Eighth Amendment: The Eighth Amendment prohibits cruel and unusual punishment and excessive fines or bail. This protection ensures that punishment for crimes is fair and proportionate.

9. Ninth Amendment: The Ninth Amendment states that the rights listed in the Constitution are not the only rights that individuals have. This amendment emphasizes that individuals have other rights not specifically mentioned in the Constitution.

10. Tenth Amendment: The Tenth Amendment reserves powers not granted to the federal government by the Constitution to the states or the people. This amendment helps maintain a balance of power between the federal government and the states.

Understanding the Constitution and the Bill of Rights is essential for any aspiring lawyer. These documents form the backbone of our legal system and serve as a guide for interpreting and applying the law. As you continue your journey into the world of law, you'll find that the Constitution and the Bill of Rights are constantly referred to in legal discussions, court cases, and legislation.

As a future lawyer, you'll play a crucial role in upholding the values and principles enshrined in the Constitution and the Bill of Rights. Whether you're advocating for your clients' rights, interpreting the law, or drafting legislation, your actions will be guided by these foundational documents. Your understanding of the Constitution and the Bill of Rights will help you navigate complex legal issues, protect individual liberties, and promote justice and fairness in society.

Now that you have a basic understanding of the Constitution and the Bill of Rights, don't stop here! There's so much more to learn about these important documents and the many ways they shape our legal system. Dive deeper into each amendment, explore landmark Supreme Court cases that have interpreted the Constitution, and discuss the principles and values embodied in these documents with your friends, family, and teachers.

landmark supreme court cases

As you continue to explore the exciting world of law, you'll undoubtedly come across some truly fascinating Supreme Court cases. These landmark cases have shaped our legal system, defined our rights, and changed the course of American history. In this section, we'll take a closer look at some of the most important and influential Supreme Court cases that every aspiring lawyer should know. Ready to dive in? Let's go!

1. Marbury v. Madison (1803)

Marbury v. Madison is one of the most significant Supreme Court cases because it established the principle of judicial review, which allows the Supreme Court to declare laws unconstitutional. This case laid the groundwork for the Court's role as the ultimate interpreter of the Constitution and helped define the balance of power between the three branches of government.

2. Brown v. Board of Education (1954)

Brown v. Board of Education was a groundbreaking case that tackled the issue of racial segregation in public schools. The Supreme Court unanimously ruled that "separate but equal" facilities were inherently unequal, and that racial segregation in public schools violated the 14th Amendment's guarantee of equal protection under the law. This decision marked a major milestone in the civil rights movement and paved the way for integration in schools across the country.

3. Miranda v. Arizona (1966)

Miranda v. Arizona is a landmark case that transformed the way police interact with criminal suspects. The Supreme Court ruled that suspects must be informed of their rights, including the right to remain silent and the right to have an attorney present during questioning. These rights, known as "Miranda rights," help protect individuals from self-incrimination and ensure that they are aware of their constitutional protections.

4. Roe v. Wade (1973)

Roe v. Wade is a highly controversial case that addressed the issue of abortion rights. The Supreme Court held that a woman's right to have an abortion is protected under the constitutional right to privacy. This landmark decision effectively legalized abortion across the United States, and it continues to be a hotly debated topic to this day.

5. United States v. Nixon (1974)

In United States v. Nixon, the Supreme Court played a crucial role in bringing about the resignation of President Richard Nixon. The Court unanimously ruled that the president could not claim executive privilege to withhold evidence in a criminal investigation. This decision reinforced the principle that no one, not even the president, is above the law.

6. Obergefell v. Hodges (2015)

Obergefell v. Hodges is a landmark case that made marriage equality the law of the land. The Supreme Court ruled that the 14th Amendment guarantees same-sex couples the right to marry, and that states must recognize and perform same-sex marriages. This historic decision marked a significant victory for LGBTQ+ rights and equality.

These are just a few of the many landmark Supreme Court cases that have shaped our legal system and defined the rights and liberties we enjoy today. As a future lawyer, it's essential to understand the importance of these cases and the profound impact they've had on our society.

By studying these landmark cases, you'll gain a

deeper appreciation for the role of the Supreme Court in interpreting and applying the Constitution. You'll also develop critical thinking skills that will serve you well as you navigate the complex world of law.

As you continue to learn about the law and explore these landmark cases, don't be afraid to ask questions, engage in discussions, and share your thoughts with others. Your curiosity and passion for learning will be your greatest assets as you work towards your goal of becoming a lawyer.

Always remember that the law is constantly evolving, and as a future lawyer, you'll play a crucial role in shaping and interpreting the legal landscape. By understanding the significance of landmark Supreme Court cases and their impact on our legal system, you'll be better prepared to advocate for your clients, protect their rights, and contribute to the ongoing evolution of the law.

So keep on learning, exploring, and questioning as you delve deeper into these influential cases and the many others that have shaped our legal system. Stay curious, be open-minded, and never stop expanding your knowledge. The more you learn about the law, the better equipped you'll be to make a real difference in the lives of your future clients and society as a whole.

As you look back on these landmark Supreme Court cases, remember that each one started with a single person who faced a legal challenge and decided to take a stand. Just like these individuals, you have the potential to change the course of history and make a lasting impact on the world through your work as a lawyer.

3 /
law school and beyond

high school preparation

AS YOU MOVE CLOSER to your goal of becoming a legal professional, it's essential to start planning and preparing for the journey ahead. High school is a crucial time for building a strong foundation in the subjects and skills that will serve you well in your legal career. In this section, we'll discuss some tips and strategies for making the most of your high school years and setting yourself up for success in the world of law. Ready to get started? Let's go!

1. Focus on core subjects

High school is an excellent opportunity to build a solid foundation in the subjects that are crucial for a career in law. Focus on developing strong skills in English, social studies, and history. These subjects will help you improve your reading, writing, and critical thinking skills, all of which are essential for aspiring lawyers. Additionally, consider taking courses in government or civics to gain a deeper understanding of the legal system and the role of lawyers in society.

2. Hone your writing skills

As a lawyer, you'll spend a significant amount of time writing, whether it's drafting legal documents, crafting persuasive arguments, or composing letters to clients. High school is a great time to refine your writing skills by taking advanced English courses, participating in writing clubs or workshops, and seeking feedback from teachers and peers.

3. Develop your public speaking abilities

Public speaking is another critical skill for lawyers, as you'll need to present your case convincingly in court and communicate effectively with clients and colleagues. Joining a debate team, participating in mock trial competitions, or taking a public speaking course can help you become a more confident and persuasive speaker.

4. Challenge yourself with advanced coursework

To succeed in law school and beyond, you'll need to develop strong analytical and problem-solving skills. Challenging yourself with advanced coursework in high school, such as Advanced Placement (AP) or International Baccalaureate (IB) classes, can help you build these skills and prepare for the rigor of college and law school.

5. Get involved in extracurricular activities

Extracurricular activities can provide valuable experiences that will help you grow as a person and stand out when applying to college and law school. Look for clubs and organizations related to law, such as mock trial, debate, or Model United Nations. These activities can help you develop a deeper understanding of the legal system and give you a taste of what it's like to be a lawyer.

6. Volunteer and gain real-world experience

Volunteering is an excellent way to gain real-world experience and make a positive impact on your community. Look for opportunities to volunteer at local legal aid clinics, courthouses, or nonprofit organizations that focus on issues you're passionate about. These experiences can help you gain a better understanding of the legal profession and demonstrate your commitment to serving others.

7. Start networking early

Building a professional network is crucial for any aspiring lawyer. Start networking early by connecting with your teachers, mentors, and peers who share your interest in law. Attend local events and workshops related to the legal field to meet professionals and learn more about the profession. Networking can help you gain valuable insights, advice, and connections that will benefit you throughout your legal career.

8. Plan for college and beyond

As you progress through high school, start researching colleges and universities that offer strong pre-law programs or have a history of success in placing students in law school. Keep track of application deadlines, requirements, and scholarship opportunities. Planning ahead will ensure that you're well-prepared to make a smooth transition from high school to college and eventually to law school.

By following these tips and making the most of your high school years, you'll be well on your way to achieving your dream of becoming a lawyer. Remember that success in the legal profession requires dedication, perseverance, and a genuine passion for the law. Stay focused on your goals, continue to challenge yourself, and never be afraid to ask for help or guidance along the way.

As you wrap up your time in high school, remember to celebrate your achievements and cherish the friendships and memories you've made. The skills, experiences, and connections you've gained during this time will serve as a strong foundation for your future legal career.

Finally, don't forget to enjoy the journey! Becoming a lawyer is a long and challenging process, but it's also incredibly rewarding. As you progress through college and law school, stay open to new experiences, continue learning, and always strive to be the best version of yourself. With hard work, determination, and a positive attitude, there's no limit to what you can achieve in the world of law.

college and choosing a major

While many aspiring lawyers often think they need to major in pre-law or political science, the truth is that there's no one-size-fits-all approach to selecting a major that will prepare you for law school and a legal career. In this section, we'll explore some tips and strategies for choosing a college major that aligns with your interests, strengths, and goals. Ready? Let's dive in!

1. Focus on your passions and interests

While it's essential to consider how your major will prepare you for law school, it's also crucial to choose a subject that genuinely interests you. College is a time for exploration and growth, and you'll be more likely to excel in your studies if you're passionate about the material. Reflect on your favorite high school courses, extracurricular activities, and personal interests to identify potential majors that align with your passions.

2. Consider majors that develop essential skills

As a lawyer, you'll need strong critical thinking,

research, writing, and communication skills. Look for majors that will help you develop these essential abilities. Some popular options among aspiring lawyers include English, history, political science, philosophy, and economics. However, don't be afraid to consider majors outside of the humanities and social sciences. Law schools value diversity, and students from fields like engineering, mathematics, and the natural sciences can also make exceptional lawyers.

3. Research law school requirements

While there's no specific undergraduate major required for law school admission, some schools may have certain course prerequisites or recommendations. Familiarize yourself with the requirements and recommendations of the law schools you're interested in attending to ensure you're on the right track.

4. Double major or minor in a related field

If you have multiple interests or want to broaden your skill set, consider pursuing a double major or minoring in a related field. For example, you might major in English and minor in political science, or double major in philosophy and economics. This approach can provide you with a well-rounded education and demonstrate your versatility and intellectual curiosity to law school admissions committees.

5. Seek guidance from academic advisors and mentors

Choosing a major can be a challenging decision, so don't hesitate to seek guidance from academic advisors, professors, and other mentors. They can help you explore your interests, identify potential majors, and provide valuable insights into the skills and experiences that will best prepare you for law school and a legal career.

6. Explore law-related courses and extracurricular activities

In addition to choosing a major, take advantage of opportunities to explore law-related courses and extracurricular activities during your college years. Courses in constitutional law, criminal justice, or legal philosophy can provide valuable insights into the legal system and help you build a strong foundation for law school. Participating in extracurricular activities like mock trial, debate, or legal internships can also help you gain practical experience and further develop your interest in the law.

7. Keep an open mind and be willing to change

As you progress through your college journey, it's essential to remain open to new experiences and be willing to adapt your plans as needed. You may discover new passions or interests that lead you to change your major, or you might find that your chosen major isn't the best fit for your goals. Be open to change, and don't be afraid to make adjustments to your plans as you learn and grow.

By following these tips and staying true to your passions and interests, you'll be well on your way to choosing a college major that prepares you for a successful legal career. Remember, there's no one "right" major for aspiring lawyers, and the most important thing is to find a subject that truly resonates with you and helps you develop the skills you'll need as a lawyer.

As you approach the end of your college journey, take time to reflect on the knowledge and skills you've gained through your major and other experiences. These will serve as a strong foundation for your future legal education and career.

Now that you have some ideas for selecting a college major, it's time to start researching and applying to colleges that align with your goals and interests. Look for schools that offer strong programs in your desired major, as well as opportunities for law-related extracurricular activities and internships. And remember, college is about more than just academics— it's also a time for personal growth, making new friends, and creating lasting memories.

Once you've chosen a major and settled into college life, continue to seek out opportunities to learn and grow both inside and outside the classroom. Engage with your professors, attend guest lectures, join clubs and organizations, and make the most of your college experience. All of these experiences will not only enrich your life but also help you develop the skills, knowledge, and connections you'll need to succeed in law school and beyond.

As you continue on your path toward becoming a lawyer, remember to stay focused on your goals, but also remain open to new experiences and opportunities. The world of law is vast and varied, and the best lawyers are those who can adapt, learn, and grow throughout their careers.

law school and the admissions process

By now, you've completed high school, chosen a college major, and gained valuable experiences that have prepared you for the next exciting step in your journey: law school. In this section, we'll explore the law school admissions process, including important factors to consider, how to prepare for the LSAT, and tips for crafting a compelling application. Let's get started!

1. Researching law schools

The first step in the law school admissions process is researching potential schools. Consider factors such as location, size, reputation, areas of specialization, and cost. Talk to current law students, alumni, and professors to get a sense of each school's culture and opportunities. Keep in mind that you'll be spending three years of your life at law school, so it's important to find a place where you'll feel challenged, supported, and inspired.

2. Preparing for the Law School Admission Test (LSAT)

The LSAT is a standardized test required for admission to most law schools in the United States. It measures your reading comprehension, analytical reasoning, and logical reasoning skills. The LSAT is a critical factor in law school admissions, so it's essential to invest time and effort into preparing for the exam. Consider using study guides, attending prep courses, or joining a study group. Give yourself plenty of time to study, practice, and become familiar with the test format.

3. Crafting a standout application

Your law school application is your opportunity to showcase your unique experiences, achievements, and aspirations. Be sure to include the following components:

- Personal statement: The personal statement is a crucial part of your application, as it allows you to share your story, motivations, and goals. Be honest, thoughtful, and genuine in your writing. Reflect on your experiences and explain how they have shaped your interest in the law and your desire to become a lawyer.

- Letters of recommendation: Choose recommenders who know you well and can speak to your strengths, character, and potential. This might include professors, employers, or mentors. Give them plenty of notice and provide them with any necessary materials to help them write a strong and informed recommendation.

- Resume: Your resume should highlight your academic achievements, work experience, extracurricular activities, and any awards or honors you've received. Be concise and focus on experiences that demonstrate your skills, leadership, and commitment to the law.

- Transcripts: Law schools will require your undergraduate transcripts as part of your application. Be sure to request these well in advance of any deadlines.

4. The interview process

Some law schools may require or offer interviews as part of the admissions process. These interviews can be an opportunity to showcase your personality, passion, and drive. Prepare by researching common interview questions and practicing your responses. Be ready to discuss your experiences, interests, and motivations for pursuing a legal career.

5. Deciding on a law school

Once you've received your admissions decisions, it's time to choose a law school. Take your time to weigh the pros and cons of each option, considering factors like financial aid packages, location, and program offerings. Talk to current students, alumni, and faculty to get a sense of each school's culture and resources. Ultimately, choose the school that you believe will best support your growth and success as a future lawyer.

6. Celebrate your achievements

Before diving into the demanding world of law school, take a moment to celebrate your accomplishments. Getting into law school is a significant achievement and a testament to your hard work, dedication, and passion for the law. Remember to thank those who have supported you along the way and be proud of all that you've accomplished thus far.

As you embark on your law school journey, keep in mind that the path ahead will be challenging, but also incredibly rewarding. You'll be learning from some of the brightest minds in the legal field and engaging with complex and fascinating legal issues. Embrace the challenges, stay curious, and remember that every step of the way, you're building the foundation for a successful legal career.

7. Tips for thriving in law school

Once you've settled into law school, it's essential to

develop effective study habits, time management skills, and a support network to help you succeed. Here are a few tips to keep in mind:

- Stay organized: Use a planner or calendar to keep track of assignments, exams, and important dates. This will help you manage your time effectively and stay on top of your workload.

- Participate in class: Engage in class discussions, ask questions, and challenge yourself to think critically about the material. Active participation will not only help you better understand the concepts, but also demonstrate your commitment and enthusiasm for the subject matter.

- Develop strong study habits: Find a study routine that works best for you, whether that's studying alone, with a group, or a combination of both. Experiment with different study techniques, such as outlining, flashcards, or teaching the material to a friend.

- Seek support: Law school can be challenging, both academically and emotionally. Don't hesitate to seek support from professors, classmates, academic advisors, or even mental health professionals. Remember that you're not alone, and it's okay to ask for help.

- Get involved: Join clubs, organizations, or moot court competitions to meet like-minded peers, gain hands-on experience, and build a strong network of connections that will serve you well throughout your career.

As you progress through law school, always remember why you chose this path in the first place. Keep your passion for the law and your desire to make a difference at the forefront of your mind. This will help motivate you through the tough times and remind you of the impact you can have as a lawyer.

passing the bar exam and becoming a licensed attorney

You've made it through law school, and now you're just one crucial step away from becoming a licensed attorney: passing the bar exam. This section will guide you through the process of preparing for and taking the bar exam, as well as exploring the steps to becoming a licensed attorney. Let's dive in!

1. Understanding the bar exam

The bar exam is a comprehensive test that assesses your knowledge of the law and your ability to apply it in real-life situations. It's a crucial milestone on your journey to becoming a lawyer, as you must pass the exam to practice law in most states. The format and content of the bar exam can vary depending on where you plan to practice, but it typically consists of multiple-choice questions, essay questions, and performance tests.

2. Preparing for the bar exam

Passing the bar exam requires dedication, focus, and plenty of preparation. Here are some tips to help you prepare effectively:

- Develop a study schedule: Create a study plan that covers all the topics you need to review, with ample time for practice questions and tests. Stick to your schedule and prioritize your study time to ensure you're fully prepared.

- Use study materials: Take advantage of the many resources available to help you prepare for the bar exam, such as bar review courses, textbooks, and online study aids. These materials can help you learn the law, practice your skills, and familiarize yourself with the exam format.

- Practice, practice, practice: The more practice questions and tests you complete, the more comfortable and confident you'll feel on exam day. Practice will help you identify areas where you need to improve and fine-tune your test-taking strategies.

- Stay healthy and manage stress: While preparing for the bar exam can be intense, it's essential to take care of yourself both physically and mentally. Exercise regularly, eat well, get enough sleep, and find ways to manage stress, such as meditation, deep breathing, or talking to friends and family.

3. Taking the bar exam

When it's time to take the bar exam, keep these strategies in mind:

- Manage your time wisely: Allocate your time effectively during the exam, making sure to pace yourself and not spend too much time on any one question.

- Read questions carefully: Be sure to read each question thoroughly, as missing a key detail can lead to an incorrect answer.

- Stay confident: Trust your preparation and believe in your ability to pass the exam. Stay focused, positive, and do your best.

4. Receiving your results

After taking the bar exam, you'll need to wait for your results, which can take several weeks or even months. Be patient, and try to stay positive during this time. When you receive your results, celebrate your accomplishments, regardless of the outcome. Remember that many successful lawyers didn't pass the bar exam on their first attempt, so don't be too hard on yourself if you need to retake the exam.

5. Becoming a licensed attorney

Once you've passed the bar exam, there are a few more steps you'll need to complete before becoming a licensed attorney:

- Character and fitness evaluation: Most states require a character and fitness evaluation to ensure that you have the moral and ethical qualities necessary to practice law. This may involve background checks, interviews, or other assessments.

- Swearing-in ceremony: After you've met all the requirements, you'll be invited to attend a swearing-in ceremony, where you'll take an oath to uphold the law and the Constitution. This is an important and exciting milestone in your journey, so be sure to invite friends and family to share in your accomplishment!

- Continuing legal education: As a licensed attorney, you'll need to stay up-to-date with changes in the law and legal practice by completing continuing legal education (CLE) courses. These courses help you maintain your skills and knowledge, ensuring that you remain an effective advocate for your clients.

- Joining professional organizations: Becoming a member of professional legal organizations, such as the American Bar Association or local bar associations, can provide you with valuable networking opportunities, access to resources, and the chance to get involved in your legal community.

6. Finding your first job as a lawyer

Now that you're a licensed attorney, it's time to find your first job in the legal field. Here are some tips to help you in your job search:

- Network: Connect with alumni, professors, and other professionals in the legal field to learn about job openings and get advice on job searching.

- Tailor your resume and cover letter: Customize your application materials to highlight your relevant skills, experiences, and accomplishments for each position you apply for.

- Prepare for interviews: Research the law firms or organizations you're interviewing with, practice answering common interview questions, and be prepared to discuss your experiences, accomplishments, and passion for the law.

- Stay persistent: The job market can be competitive, so stay persistent and keep applying to positions, even if you face rejection. Your determination and hard work will pay off in the end.

As you embark on your career as a licensed attorney, remember to stay true to your passion for the law and your commitment to making a difference in the world. Embrace the challenges and rewards of your chosen profession, and never stop learning and growing as a lawyer.

You've come a long way on your journey to becoming a lawyer, and passing the bar exam and becoming a licensed attorney is a significant accomplishment. Always remember the hard work, dedication, and passion that got you to this point, and use those qualities to make a difference in the lives of your clients and your community. The world needs more skilled, compassionate, and dedicated lawyers like you, so go forth and make your mark on the legal profession!

4 /
careers in law

types of legal careers

NOW THAT YOU'VE learned about the path to becoming a lawyer, it's time to explore the different types of legal careers available. There's a whole world of possibilities out there, and each career path has its unique challenges and rewards. In this section, we'll introduce you to some of the most common legal careers, so you can start thinking about which one might be the best fit for you!

1. Litigation Attorney

Litigation attorneys represent clients in court, handling a wide range of civil and criminal cases. These lawyers are skilled in trial advocacy, negotiation, and legal research and writing. They may work on cases involving personal injury, contracts, property disputes, or criminal defense, among other areas. If you enjoy the excitement and challenge of the courtroom, a career as a litigation attorney might be perfect for you.

2. Corporate Attorney

Corporate attorneys work with businesses to help them navigate complex legal issues related to their operations. They may advise on topics like mergers and acquisitions, corporate governance, securities law, and intellectual property. Corporate attorneys often work for large law firms or as in-house counsel for corporations. If you have an interest in business and finance, a career as a corporate attorney could be a great fit.

3. Intellectual Property Attorney

Intellectual property (IP) attorneys specialize in protecting the rights of creators and inventors. They work on cases involving patents, trademarks, copyrights, and trade secrets. IP attorneys help clients secure their rights to inventions, creative works, and brand names. If you have a passion for innovation and creativity, a career as an IP attorney might be right up your alley.

4. Family Law Attorney

Family law attorneys focus on legal issues related to families, such as divorce, child custody, adoption, and guardianship. They help clients navigate sensitive and emotional situations while ensuring their rights are protected. If you have a strong desire to help people through difficult times, a career in family law might be a rewarding choice.

5. Environmental Law Attorney

Environmental law attorneys work on cases related to the environment, natural resources, and wildlife protection. They may represent clients in disputes over pollution, land use, or conservation. Environmental lawyers might work for government agencies, nonprofit organizations, or private law firms. If you're passionate about protecting the environment and preserving our natural resources, a career in environmental law could be a perfect fit.

6. Immigration Attorney

Immigration attorneys help individuals and families navigate the complex process of immigrating to a new country. They may assist with visa applications, work permits, and citizenship matters. Immigration attorneys also represent clients in deportation proceedings and asylum cases. If you have a strong sense of compassion and a desire to help people build a better life, a career in immigration law might be a great choice for you.

7. Criminal Defense Attorney

Criminal defense attorneys represent individuals who have been accused of committing crimes. They work to ensure that their clients receive a fair trial and that their legal rights are protected throughout the criminal justice process. Criminal defense attorneys may work on cases involving minor offenses, like traffic violations, or more serious crimes, such as robbery or murder. If you're passionate about justice and believe in the importance of a fair legal system, a career as a criminal defense attorney could be a rewarding path.

8. Civil Rights Attorney

Civil rights attorneys work to protect the rights and liberties of individuals and groups who face discrimination or unfair treatment. They may represent clients in cases involving issues like voting rights, racial or gender discrimination, or police misconduct. Civil rights attorneys often work for nonprofit organizations, government agencies, or private law firms. If you're passionate about social justice and equality, a career as a civil rights attorney could be an excellent fit for you.

9. Employment and Labor Law Attorney

Employment and labor law attorneys specialize in cases related to the workplace. They may represent employees who have been wrongfully terminated, discriminated against, or harassed on the job. They might also work with employers to ensure compliance with labor laws and to handle employee disputes. If you have an interest in workplace rights and the relationship between employers and employees, a career in employment and labor law might be a great choice.

10. Estate Planning Attorney

Estate planning attorneys help individuals and families plan for the future, including the distribution of assets after death. They assist clients in drafting wills, trusts, and other legal documents and may also handle cases involving probate and estate administration. If you have an interest in helping people plan for their futures and navigate the complexities of inheritance, a career as an estate planning attorney could be a great fit.

As you can see, there are many different types of legal careers to choose from, each with its unique challenges and rewards. It's important to think about your passions and interests as you explore these options and consider which path might be the best fit for you. Remember that the legal profession is diverse and ever-changing, so there will always be new opportunities to learn, grow, and make a difference in the world as a lawyer.

choosing your area of specialization

Choosing a specialization is an important decision, as it can shape your career path and determine the types of cases you'll handle throughout your professional life.

In this section, we'll discuss some helpful tips and strategies for selecting the right area of law for you. Let's get started!

1. Identify Your Interests and Passions

The first step in choosing a specialization is to think about what truly excites and motivates you. Are you passionate about protecting the environment? Do you have a strong sense of justice and a desire to help those who have been wronged? Perhaps you're drawn to the world of business and finance, or maybe you love learning about the intricacies of intellectual property law. Make a list of your interests and passions, and use this as a starting point to narrow down your options.

2. Consider Your Skills and Strengths

Next, think about your unique skills and strengths. Are you a natural problem-solver who excels at finding creative solutions? Maybe you're an excellent communicator who can present complex ideas in a clear and concise manner. Or perhaps you have a knack for negotiation and building consensus among opposing parties. Reflect on your abilities and how they might align with different areas of law. This can help you identify potential specializations that will allow you to excel and make the most of your talents.

3. Research Different Areas of Law

Once you have a better understanding of your interests, passions, skills, and strengths, it's time to start researching different areas of law more in-depth. Read books, articles, and blogs about various legal fields, and consider attending lectures or workshops in your community. You might even want to reach out to lawyers who practice in the areas you're considering and ask them about their experiences. The more you learn about each area of law, the better equipped you'll be to make an informed decision about your specialization.

4. Shadow or Intern with a Lawyer

Another great way to explore different areas of law is to shadow or intern with a lawyer who practices in a field you're considering. This hands-on experience can give you a firsthand look at the day-to-day work of a lawyer in a specific area and help you determine if it's a good fit for you. You'll also have the opportunity to ask questions, observe real cases, and build valuable connections in the legal community.

5. Think About Your Career Goals

As you explore different areas of law, it's important to consider your long-term career goals. Are you hoping to work for a large law firm or a nonprofit organization? Do you want to become an in-house counsel for a corporation, or do you dream of opening your own practice? Consider how each area of law aligns with your goals and aspirations, and use this information to guide your decision-making process.

6. Attend Law School Classes or Workshops

If you're still unsure about which area of law to specialize in, attending law school classes or workshops can be an excellent way to gain more insight into your options. These educational opportunities can introduce you to the foundational concepts of various legal fields and help you determine which areas are most appealing to you. Plus, you'll have the chance to engage with other students and professors, who can offer valuable advice and guidance on choosing a specialization.

7. Keep an Open Mind

Remember that choosing a specialization isn't set in stone. Many lawyers change their focus or explore new areas of law throughout their careers, so don't feel pressured to make a final decision right away. Be open to new experiences and opportunities, and give yourself the freedom to change your mind if you discover a different area of law that feels like a better fit. The legal profession is vast and ever-evolving, so it's important to stay adaptable and open to change.

8. Seek Mentorship and Guidance

As you navigate the process of choosing a specialization, it's important to have a support system in place. Reach out to experienced lawyers, professors, or even fellow students who can offer advice and guidance based on their own experiences. Don't be afraid to ask questions and seek feedback from those around you. The insights and perspectives of others can be incredibly valuable in helping you make the best decision for your future.

9. Reflect on Your Personal Values

In addition to considering your interests, skills, and career goals, it's essential to think about your personal values and how they align with different areas of law. Some areas of law may involve working with clients or organizations that don't share your values, while others might allow you to advocate for causes you deeply believe in. Reflect on what's most important to you and how your chosen specialization can help you live in alignment with your values.

10. Give Yourself Time

Finally, remember that choosing a specialization is a significant decision, and it's okay to take your time. You may not have all the answers right away, and that's perfectly normal. As you progress through your education and gain more experience in the legal world, your interests and passions may evolve, leading you to new areas of law that you hadn't previously considered. Trust the process, and know that with time and patience, you'll find the right specialization for you.

balancing work, family, and community involvement

Have you ever tried to juggle a bunch of different objects at once? It's not easy, right? Well, that's kind of what life can be like sometimes, especially when you're a lawyer. Between work, family, and community involvement, it can feel like you're juggling a whole bunch of responsibilities all at once. But don't worry! With the right strategies and a little bit of practice, you can learn how to balance everything and keep all those balls in the air. In this section, we'll share some tips and tricks for achieving a healthy balance between work, family, and community involvement as a lawyer.

1. Set Realistic Goals and Priorities

The first step to finding balance is setting realistic goals and priorities for yourself. It's important to recognize that you can't do everything, so you'll need to figure out what's most important to you. Start by making a list of your priorities in work, family, and community involvement. This will help you see where you need to focus your time and energy.

2. Create a Schedule

Once you have a clear idea of your priorities, it's time to create a schedule to help you manage your time effectively. Make sure to include time for work, family, and community involvement, as well as some downtime for yourself. Remember, it's essential to have some time to relax and recharge, so don't forget to schedule some "me time" as well.

3. Set Boundaries

Setting boundaries is crucial when it comes to balancing work, family, and community involvement. It's important to know when to say "no" and to protect your personal time. For example, if you've set aside time to spend with your family, try to avoid checking work emails or taking work calls during that time. By setting boundaries, you can ensure that you're giving each area of your life the attention it deserves.

4. Learn to Delegate and Ask for Help

You don't have to do everything by yourself! One of the best ways to find balance is to learn how to delegate tasks and ask for help when you need it. At work, consider delegating tasks to colleagues or support staff when your workload is overwhelming. At home, don't be afraid to ask family members for help with chores or other responsibilities. Remember, it's okay to lean on others when you need support.

5. Make Time for Your Health and Well-being

When you're busy juggling work, family, and community involvement, it's easy to let your health and well-being fall by the wayside. But taking care of yourself is essential for maintaining balance and preventing burnout. Make sure to eat well, get regular exercise, and prioritize sleep. It's also important to find ways to manage stress, whether that's through meditation, yoga, or other relaxation techniques.

6. Stay Organized

Staying organized can make a big difference when it comes to balancing work, family, and community involvement. Keep track of important dates, deadlines, and events using a calendar or planner. Make to-do lists to help you stay on top of tasks and responsibilities. The more organized you are, the easier it will be to manage your time effectively and find balance.

7. Communicate with Your Family

Communication is key when it comes to finding balance between work, family, and community involvement. Talk to your family members about your schedule and make sure they understand your commitments. This will help you avoid misunderstandings and ensure that everyone is on the same page.

8. Be Flexible

Life can be unpredictable, and sometimes things don't go according to plan. It's important to be flexible and adaptable when it comes to balancing work, family, and community involvement. If something unexpected comes up, be willing to adjust your schedule and make changes as needed. Remember, finding balance isn't about sticking to a rigid routine;

it's about being able to adapt and find harmony amidst the chaos.

9. Prioritize Quality Time

When you're busy juggling work, family, and community involvement, it can be easy to let the time you spend with your loved ones slip away. Make sure to prioritize quality time with your family, even if it means making small adjustments to your schedule. Whether it's sharing a meal together, playing a game, or going for a walk, these moments are essential for maintaining strong relationships and keeping your life balanced.

10. Celebrate Your Accomplishments

Lastly, don't forget to celebrate your accomplishments along the way! Balancing work, family, and community involvement is no small feat, and it's important to recognize the progress you're making. Take time to acknowledge your achievements, both big and small, and be proud of the balance you're creating in your life.

Finding the perfect balance between work, family, and community involvement can be challenging, especially for busy lawyers. But with the right strategies and a little

5 /
conclusion

the rewards of being a lawyer

GUESS WHAT? There's a big secret about being a lawyer that not many people know about. Are you ready for it? Here it is: being a lawyer can be incredibly rewarding! Sure, you might have heard that lawyers work long hours and deal with stressful situations, but there are also many amazing benefits to this profession. In this section, we'll explore some of the most rewarding aspects of being a lawyer. Get ready to be inspired!

1. Making a Difference

One of the most rewarding parts of being a lawyer is the ability to make a real difference in people's lives. Lawyers have the power to help their clients navigate complex legal situations, protect their rights, and achieve justice. Whether you're helping someone fight for their rights, resolve a dispute, or defend themselves in court, it's an incredible feeling to know that your work has a positive impact on someone's life.

2. Intellectual Challenge

If you love puzzles and problem-solving, you'll find the intellectual challenges of being a lawyer particularly rewarding. The law is like a giant puzzle, with many different pieces that need to be put together to create a complete picture. Lawyers must analyze complex legal issues, find creative solutions, and make persuasive arguments. It's like playing a challenging game of chess, where you need to use your wits and strategy to outsmart your opponent.

3. Variety and Excitement

No two days are the same when you're a lawyer! Each case you work on is unique, and you'll encounter a wide variety of legal issues throughout your career. This means that you're always learning something new and facing exciting challenges. Plus, you might have the opportunity to work in different areas of the law, which can keep your work fresh and engaging.

4. Job Security and Financial Rewards

Lawyers are often in high demand, which means that you'll have good job security in this profession.

Plus, the financial rewards of being a lawyer can be quite attractive. While not all lawyers make a fortune, many do earn a comfortable living, which can provide financial stability for you and your family.

5. Prestige and Respect

Being a lawyer is considered a prestigious profession, and people often hold lawyers in high regard. You might find that your friends and family are impressed by your accomplishments and look up to you as a role model. While it's not the most important reward of being a lawyer, it's still nice to be respected for your hard work and dedication.

6. Opportunities for Personal and Professional Growth

As a lawyer, you'll have countless opportunities for personal and professional growth. You'll develop strong communication, negotiation, and critical thinking skills, which can be applied to many aspects of your life. Plus, you'll have the chance to network with other professionals and expand your knowledge of the law by attending conferences, workshops, and continuing education courses.

7. Flexibility

While many lawyers work in traditional law firms, there are also many different ways to practice law. You might choose to work for a government agency, a non-profit organization, or even start your own law practice. This flexibility allows you to find a career path that aligns with your values and interests, making your work even more rewarding.

8. The Power of Knowledge

As a lawyer, you'll have a deep understanding of the law and how it affects people's lives. This knowledge can be incredibly empowering, as it allows you to navigate the legal system with confidence and help others do the same. Plus, you'll be able to use your legal expertise to advocate for changes in the law and contribute to the greater good.

9. Teamwork and Collaboration

Although lawyers are often portrayed as lone wolves, the reality is that many lawyers work as part of a team. Collaborating with colleagues, working with support staff, and partnering with experts in other fields can be a rewarding aspect of the profession. This teamwork not only allows you to learn from others and expand your skillset, but it also fosters a sense of camaraderie and support that can make your work even more enjoyable.

10. Building Relationships

As a lawyer, you'll have the opportunity to build relationships with a diverse group of people, including clients, colleagues, and other professionals. These relationships can be incredibly rewarding, as you help your clients through difficult times and work together to achieve their goals. Plus, the connections you make in your professional life can lead to lasting friendships and a strong support network.

11. Sense of Accomplishment

Finally, one of the most rewarding aspects of being a lawyer is the sense of accomplishment that comes from successfully resolving a case or helping a client achieve their goals. When you see the positive impact of your work on someone's life, it's hard not to feel a sense of pride and satisfaction. It's moments like these that make all the hard work and long hours worth it.

lifelong learning and growth in the legal profession

Alright, future lawyers, let's talk about something really important: lifelong learning and growth in the legal profession. Did you know that even after you've finished law school, passed the bar exam, and started working as a lawyer, you'll still have plenty of opportunities to learn and grow? That's right! A career in law is all about constantly expanding your knowledge and improving your skills, which makes it an exciting and dynamic field to be a part of. Let's explore some of the ways you'll continue to learn and grow throughout your legal career.

1. Staying Updated on Legal Developments

The world of law is always changing. New laws are enacted, existing laws are amended, and important court decisions are made that can impact how the law is interpreted and applied. As a lawyer, it's crucial to stay updated on these developments so you can provide the best possible advice and representation to your clients. This means regularly reading legal journals, attending seminars and conferences, and staying informed about news and events related to your area of practice.

2. Continuing Legal Education (CLE)

Many states require lawyers to complete a certain number of Continuing Legal Education (CLE) hours each year to maintain their license to practice law. CLE courses cover a wide range of topics, from updates on specific areas of law to new legal technologies and practice management techniques. Attending CLE courses is a great way to expand your knowledge, sharpen your skills, and stay current with the latest legal developments.

3. Networking and Professional Associations

Joining professional associations, such as your local bar association or a national organization related to your area of practice, can provide valuable opportunities for learning and growth. These groups often host events, seminars, and workshops where you can connect with other legal professionals, learn from experts in the field, and stay updated on the latest trends and issues in the legal profession.

4. Learning from Mentors and Colleagues

Throughout your legal career, you'll have the chance to work with and learn from experienced lawyers who can share their wisdom, insights, and advice. Don't be afraid to ask questions, seek guidance, and learn from the successes and challenges of others in the profession. Your colleagues can be an invaluable source of knowledge and support, helping you to grow both personally and professionally.

5. Developing New Skills

The legal profession is constantly evolving, and it's important to be adaptable and open to learning new skills. This might mean taking on new responsibilities at work, attending training sessions on emerging legal technologies, or learning about different areas of law to expand your practice. By continually challenging your-self and seeking out new learning opportunities, you'll keep your skills sharp and stay ahead of the curve in the ever-changing world of law.

6. Teaching and Mentoring Others

As you gain experience and expertise in the legal profession, you'll have the chance to give back by teaching and mentoring others. Whether it's speaking at a seminar, teaching a CLE course, or mentoring a new lawyer at your firm, sharing your knowledge with others can be incredibly rewarding and help you to solidify your own understanding of complex legal concepts.

7. Reflecting on Your Progress

Taking time to reflect on your growth and progress as a lawyer is important for maintaining a sense of purpose and direction in your career. Regularly evaluate your goals, achievements, and areas for improvement, and consider how you can continue to learn and grow in the future. This self-reflection can help you stay focused, motivated, and excited about your career in law.

8. Embracing Challenges

The legal profession can be challenging, but facing those challenges head-on can lead to significant growth and development. Embrace difficult cases, complex legal issues, and new responsibilities as opportunities to learn and grow.

9. Pro Bono Work and Community Involvement

Engaging in pro bono work and getting involved in your community can provide valuable learning experiences and contribute to your personal and professional growth. By offering free legal services to those in need or participating in community projects, you'll not only make a positive impact on the lives of others, but also gain new perspectives, develop a deeper under-standing of various legal issues, and strengthen your problem-solving skills.

10. Expanding Your Network

As you grow in your legal career, expanding your professional network can open up new opportunities for learning and collaboration. Attend industry events, conferences, and networking functions to connect with other legal professionals, share ideas, and learn from their experiences. By fostering strong relationships with your peers, you'll gain access to a wealth of knowledge and resources that can help you further develop your skills and expertise.

11. Pursuing Advanced Degrees or Certifications

Some lawyers choose to pursue advanced degrees or certifications to deepen their knowledge and specialize in a particular area of law. For example, you might consider obtaining a Master of Laws (LL.M.) in a specific field, such as tax law or environmental law, or earning a certification from a professional organization related to your practice area. Pursuing additional education can help you become an expert in your chosen field and lead to new professional opportunities.

12. Embracing a Growth Mindset

Throughout your legal career, it's important to

maintain a growth mindset – the belief that your abilities can be developed through hard work, dedication, and perseverance. By embracing challenges, learning from mistakes, and viewing setbacks as opportunities for growth, you'll be better equipped to navigate the ups and downs of the legal profession and continue to thrive in your career.

inspiring quotes from famous lawyers and judges

Sometimes, a little bit of inspiration can go a long way, especially when it comes from those who have walked the path before us. In this section, we'll take a look at some inspiring quotes from famous lawyers and judges throughout history. These wise words can offer guidance, motivation, and a deeper understanding of what it means to be a lawyer.

1. "The life of the law has not been logic; it has been experience." - Oliver Wendell Holmes Jr.

This quote by the renowned Supreme Court Justice reminds us that the law is a living, breathing entity shaped by the experiences and lessons learned throughout history. It is not just a set of abstract rules, but a dynamic and ever-evolving system that reflects the complexities of human life.

2. "Injustice anywhere is a threat to justice everywhere." - Martin Luther King Jr.

Though not a lawyer, Martin Luther King Jr. was a civil rights leader who fought tirelessly for justice and equality. This quote highlights the importance of addressing and correcting injustices wherever they exist, as they can have far-reaching consequences for society as a whole.

3. "Real courage is when you know you're licked before you begin, but you begin anyway and see it through no matter what." - Harper Lee

Harper Lee, the author of the classic novel "To Kill a Mockingbird," tells us through her character, the courageous lawyer Atticus Finch, that real courage is not giving up, even when the odds are stacked against you. This quote serves as a reminder to keep fighting for what you believe in, no matter the challenges that lie ahead.

4. "The power of the lawyer is in the uncertainty of the law." - Jeremy Bentham

English philosopher and jurist Jeremy Bentham highlights the critical role lawyers play in interpreting and applying the law. With the law being complex and open to interpretation, a skilled lawyer can help bring clarity and understanding, ultimately shaping the course of justice.

5. "The first duty of society is justice." - Alexander Hamilton

One of the founding fathers of the United States, Alexander Hamilton, underscores the importance of justice as a cornerstone of a well-functioning society. Lawyers have the responsibility to help uphold this duty by representing their clients fairly and ethically.

6. "The true measure of our character is how we treat the poor, the disfavored, the accused, the incarcerated, and the condemned." - Bryan Stevenson

Civil rights lawyer and author Bryan Stevenson reminds us that our true character is revealed in how we treat the most vulnerable members of society. As lawyers, it is essential to work towards ensuring that everyone has access to justice, regardless of their circumstances.

7. "It is the spirit and not the form of law that keeps justice alive." - Earl Warren

This quote from former Chief Justice Earl Warren emphasizes the importance of the underlying principles and values that guide the law. By staying true to the spirit of the law, lawyers can ensure that justice is served and the rights of all individuals are protected.

8. "A lawyer's either a social engineer or ... a parasite on society ... A social engineer [is] a highly skilled, perceptive, sensitive lawyer who [understands] the Constitution of the United States and [knows] how to

explore its uses in the solving of problems of local communities and in bettering conditions of the under-privileged citizens." - Charles Hamilton Houston

Charles Hamilton Houston, a prominent civil rights lawyer, encourages lawyers to be social engineers who use their skills and knowledge to improve society. By embracing this mindset, lawyers can make a positive impact on the lives of others and work towards a more just and equitable world.

As we wrap up this section, let these inspiring quotes from famous lawyers and judges serve as a reminder of the critical role lawyers play in society and the importance of justice. Let them serve as motivation to pursue a career in law and make a difference in the world. Keep these wise words in mind as you embark on your journey to become a lawyer, and remember that you have the power to shape the course of justice and leave a lasting impact on the lives of others.

9. "The law is not an end in itself, nor does it provide ends. It is preeminently a means to serve what we think is right." - Justice William J. Brennan Jr.

Supreme Court Justice William J. Brennan Jr. reminds us that the law is a tool for achieving justice and fairness. As lawyers, it's essential to remember that the law is not inflexible, but a means to serve the greater good and uphold the values we believe in.

10. "The law is reason, free from passion." - Aristotle

Ancient Greek philosopher Aristotle believed that the law should be guided by reason, rather than being swayed by emotions. This quote serves as a reminder for lawyers to approach their work with a clear and unbiased mind, ensuring that decisions are made based on facts and logical reasoning.

11. "An unjust law is no law at all." - St. Augustine

St. Augustine, an early Christian theologian, emphasizes that laws must be just in order to be legitimate. This quote is a reminder that it is essential for lawyers to be vigilant and challenge unjust laws, working towards a fairer and more just legal system.

12. "Justice is the end of government. It is the end of civil society. It ever has been and ever will be pursued until it be obtained, or until liberty be lost in the pursuit." - James Madison

James Madison, one of the founding fathers of the United States, highlights the importance of pursuing justice tirelessly. As lawyers, it is essential to remain steadfast in our pursuit of justice, knowing that it is the ultimate goal of both government and civil society.

13. "The rights of one are as sacred as the rights of a million." - Eugene V. Debs

Eugene V. Debs, an American labor leader, reminds us that every individual's rights are equally important, no matter how many people they represent. This quote serves as a reminder for lawyers to treat each case with the same level of dedication and attention, regardless of the number of people affected.

As you continue your journey towards becoming a lawyer, remember that your actions have the power to shape society and create a more just and equitable world. Carry these inspiring quotes with you as you work towards making a difference in the lives of others and upholding the ideals of justice and fairness.

Milton Keynes UK
Ingram Content Group UK Ltd.
UKHW041451121024
449426UK00001B/19